D0311983

GO FACTS SEASONS

Winter

A & C BLACK • LONDON

Winter

MORAY COUNCIL LIBRARIES & INFO.SERVICES	
2O 15 59 93	
Askews	
J508.2	

© Blake Publishing 2003
Additional material © A & C Black Publishers Ltd 2005

First published 2003 in Australia by Blake Education Pty Ltd

This edition published 2005 in the United Kingdom by
A & C Black Publishers Ltd, 37 Soho Square, London W1D 3QZ
www.acblack.com

Published by permission of Blake Publishing Pty Ltd, Glebe NSW, Australia.
All rights reserved. No part of this publication may be reproduced in any form
or by any means - graphic, electronic or mechanical, including photocopying,
recording, taping or information storage and retrieval systems - without the
prior written permission of the publishers.

ISBN-10: 0-7136-7270-6
ISBN-13: 978-0-7136-7270-1

A CIP record for this book is available from the British Library.

Written by Katy Pike
Design and layout by The Modern Art Production Group
Photos by John Foxx, Photodisc, Corel, Brand X, Corbis, Digital Stock,
Rubberball, Comstock, Stockbyte, Eyewire and Artville.

UK series consultant: Julie Garnett

Printed in China by WKT Company Ltd.

A & C Black uses paper produced with elemental chlorine-free pulp,
harvested from managed sustainable forests.

Contents

Signs of Winter

As autumn turns to winter, what changes can you see and feel?

Winter is the coldest season. The sun rises later and sets earlier. The days are shorter. Winter clothes need to be thick and warm.

Sometimes it gets very cold. It may snow. Water may **freeze** on ponds, lakes and rivers.

Holly

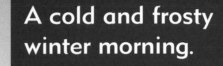

A cold and frosty winter morning.

GO FACT!

SHORTEST!
The shortest day of the year is called the winter solstice, on December 21st or 22nd.

5

Plants in Winter

Plants grow very little or not at all.

Deciduous trees have lost their leaves. The branches are bare.

Not all trees lose their leaves. Pine trees are green all year round. They are **evergreen** trees.

Some plants look like they are dead, but underground the roots and bulbs are still alive. The plants will grow again in spring.

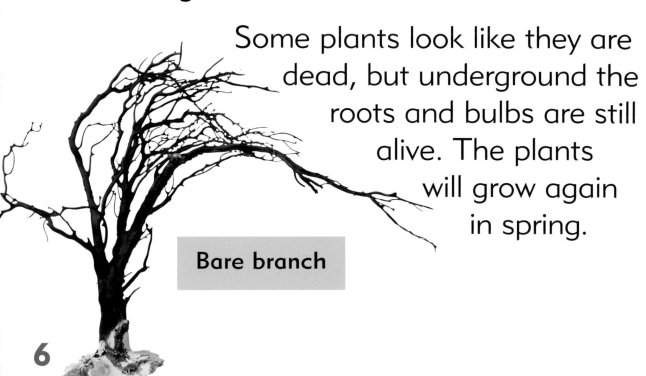

Bare branch

6

Deciduous trees have bare branches in winter.

These trees will grow new leaves in spring.

Pine needles can live even after being frozen.

In the Garden

Most plants have stopped growing.

Gardens may look empty in winter. Vegetables have been harvested and flowers picked. Some garden plants die in winter. Others stop growing until the next spring. They are **dormant**.

In warmer countries, some vegetables, like broccoli and onions, grow slowly in winter.

Gardening tools

These lily bulbs will not grow until spring.

Trees can be planted in winter.

Pruning, or trimming, plants can be done during winter.

In winter some plants can be grown indoors. 9

Winter Food

Eating hot food makes people feel warmer.

In winter, people enjoy eating hot foods, such as soups and stews. Hot porridge is a healthy winter breakfast. Cocoa makes a warm winter drink.

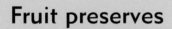
Fruit preserves

Some people enjoy **preserves** in winter. In summer, fruits such as peaches and berries can be made into jams or canned to eat all year round.

Toast with jam

10

What is your favourite kind of soup?

Stews are usually cooked for a long time.

A hot drink tastes good on a snowy day.

People in Winter

People wear warm clothes because of the cold weather.

People wear more clothes in winter. Jumpers, heavy coats, scarves and gloves help keep us warm.

There are many winter sports. Some people like playing football or hockey. Other people like skiing down snow-covered mountains.

Winter clothes

12

Children carry a sledge out to the hills.

You need waterproof gloves when you make a snowman.

GO FACT!

DID YOU KNOW?
A Norwegian skier, Bjorn Dählie, has won more Winter Olympic medals than any other person. He has 12.

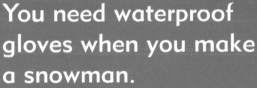

Being active keeps us warm when playing outside in winter.

13

Animals in Winter

Many animals spend more time sleeping in winter.

Border collie

Some animals **hibernate** or sleep through the winter. There are fewer plants and insects for them to eat.

Other animals like sheep, horses and dogs grow thicker coats. Some animals such as squirrels eat food they hid during summer and autumn.

Sheep and lamb

14

GO FACT!

LONGEST!
The Siberian birch mouse
hibernates for 8–9 months
every year.

Cows grow
thicker coats
in winter.

Some horses wear
turnout rugs in winter.

15

Glossary

deciduous losing leaves in autumn

dormant not growing for a while; resting

evergreen having living, green leaves for the whole year

freeze change into ice

hibernate spend the winter sleeping or resting

preserves fruit cooked with sugar and kept in jars or cans

winter the coldest part of the year

Index

16